Through the Storm
From Infertility to Supernatural Fertility

by Terriny Lloyd

Through the Storm: From Infertility to Supernatural Fertility
By: Terriny Lloyd

Copyright 2020 @ Terriny Lloyd.
Editing by Christian Cashelle, Dynamic Image Publications.
All rights reserved, including the right to reproduce this
book or portions thereof in any form whatsoever.

This book is dedicated to my mom and dad, who I love and miss dearly.

I also dedicate this book to my husband, James and my children, Haley and Adelynn. Without them, this book would not have come to fruition.

Last but not least, I also dedicate this book to all of the women who have, are, and will suffer the storm of infertility. I pray that this book blesses and inspires you.

Intro

Have you ever wanted something so bad, but you were unable to get it? Well, I have. Infertility caused me great despair and repeated disappointment. This storm cloud was so heavy that I often wondered would the storm ever end? When going through the storm of infertility, you feel as though you are the only one going through it. Even when you talk to others about it, their words are not as reassuring as you would like them to be.

Although many people knew that I experienced infertility, they never knew the extent of how it deeply wounded and affected me mentally, physically, and emotionally. This journey was a dark one that ended with a happy ending.

I always desired to be a mother, but my journey came along with a struggle. I even began to ponder if me being childless was God's plan, but I learned that was not true. My misguided identity was a struggle of me not knowing who I was or whose I was. I allowed my identity to be shaped by society and what it defined as womanhood.

Come with me as we travel through this long, tumultuous storm that wreaked havoc on so many areas in my life. It is my journey through the storm of infertility to supernatural fertility.

"Faith is the substance of things hoped for and the evidence of things not seen" - Hebrews 11:1.

Mother's Death

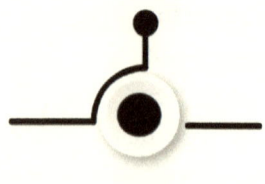

1990

Chapter 1

Joy Taken Away

I have always been the type of person that envisioned that my life would be well put together. In the beginning, it was. I lived in a modest home with my mom, dad, and siblings. There were eight of us and I was next to the youngest.

We were brought up in a loving home with great parents. My dad was an entrepreneur. He and his brothers owned a trucking company which was a really huge accomplishment back in the '80s. My dad was a serious, no-nonsense type of person. He gave respect and therefore he expected it. In spite of his serious demeanor, he was a very generous person. My father provided a really good living for our family.

My mom was a stay at home mom. She was such a sweet person and a joy to be around. She made each one of us feel special and loved. Each one of us felt that we were her favorite. Every morning, my baby sister and I couldn't wait see her face because her smile would instantaneously light up the room and our hearts. She would always welcome us with open arms. That always brought joy to my heart.

Although it seemed that things were going well, there were some issues that my mom and dad dealt with privately that ultimately lead up to their divorce. My mom and dad divorced when I was 10 years old. I can't say that I was sad, but I will say that I know it hurt my mom. I wasn't sad because this was during the time that children knew their place and that was to stay out of grown folk's business. Until this day, I cannot tell you the intricate details that led to their divorce, but I can say that our lives were never the same.

After the divorce, I can remember the look on my mother's face and all I could see was worry. She worried because a mother always wants what is best for her children and if she feels that is not possible, that can cause a deep level of concern. My mother tried her best to maintain a sense of normalcy in our lives in the midst of the uncertainty that our family was experiencing. I know that she worried about her children and how this was going to affect us.

My parent's divorce literally broke my mother's heart. She had to find a way to let go of life as she once knew it and process the reality of what life was to become. Now let me make this clear, my dad was still present and made sure that he provided for us financially. However, our lifestyle was still different. We no longer lived in a two-parent home which could pose many issues within a child such as low self-esteem and lack of confidence.

In order to compensate for our new normal in spite of what she was going through, my mom never neglected to show us love. She would always say positive things to keep us focused and inspired and to let us know that we were going to get through this.

My loving mother tried to be the best mom that she could be. Although she gave her children the best, inwardly she was struggling. She was stressed to the say the least. In a marriage, there are bonds that are created and once those bond are broken, there are fears that surface. Those fears include a threatening impact on a person's safety, security, and even survival. My mom's experience with this is what caused her stress. It not only affected her mentally, but also physically.

One day while in the car with my mom and one of my sisters, a thought crossed my mind.

"What would it be like if I lost my mother?"

As I think back, I oftentimes ponder why did such a strong and powerful thought cross a child's mind? I now know that it was discernment. I'm sad to say that thought one day became my reality.

One Sunday morning, I woke up and found it odd that my mother had yet to awaken. She was usually an early riser. I walked to her room to check on her and she was still lying in bed. So, I walked over to her bed and noticed that she appeared pale. I shook her to try and wake her up, but there was no response. I pulled her arm up and it just fell back down. Her body was cold to the touch. My mother was deceased! Calmly, I went to wake up my older siblings and told them about our mother. They began to cry hysterically. I remember just sitting and staring at her. All I could think about was that I had just lost the person that I loved the most. Have you ever loved someone more than you have ever loved yourself? Well, that is how I felt about my mom. That loss left a huge void in my life and literally broke my heart. The hurt that I experienced felt like someone ripped my heart out of my chest. My joy was taken away.

The day of my mother's funeral helped me realize that I had an inner strength that could only come from God. I did not cry and tried to remain strong for the rest of my siblings. Who does that at twelve, especially when your siblings are grown?

After the funeral and on our way to my mother's burial, it finally dawned on me that I was not going to see my mother again. I cried long and uncontrollably. I could not understand why my mom had to die so early. She was only 43. She had her whole life ahead of her.

This was my first experience with death and grief. I lost my mother at the tender age of twelve. This was my first year in middle school; a time when girls really need their moms. The loss of my mother, in turn, caused me to lose a part of me.

The death of my mom affected me in multiple ways. For one, I felt that I had to grow up quickly. No, that did not mean that I had to take care of myself. No one told me that. I just felt that I had to mature in order to deal with my current circumstances. Also, during this period, my living situation changed. One of my sisters decided to step up and become a caregiver for me and my baby sister and I appreciated her for doing that.

I will say that God placed some really great people in my life that I am forever grateful for such as my dad, siblings, and childhood friends' parents. Although I had friends and family, no one and nothing could fill the void. I just truly missed my mom.

The loss of my mom taught me a valuable lesson. I learned that God was always with me. I am reminded of the scripture in the Bible that is located in Deuteronomy 31:6:

"Be strong and courageous. Do not be afraid or terrified because of them, for the Lord your God goes with you; he will never leave you nor forsake you."

This scripture describes my life. I know that God placed an inner strength inside of me that gave me courage and the ability to withstand any obstacle that I faced. I can also confidently say that God has always been by my side every step of the way.

1995

**Graduated
High School**

Chapter 2

Not Graduating; Not an Option

After graduation from high school in 1995, I enrolled at Tougaloo College, a HBCU in Mississippi. It was a school that was known for its high graduation rate of pre-med students. Ever since I was a child, I had aspired to become a pediatrician. I had a deep passion for wanting to help children.

College was a really intimidating experience for me. It was my first time being away from home. It was also scary because I had to open up and be willing to meet people and make new friends. This was not something that I was comfortable doing due to my mild-mannered and shy demeanor.

After I arrived on campus, I immediately became nervous and anxious. My siblings and dad knew how I felt and suggested that my baby sister stay with me the entire week. I was so grateful for that because I was just not ready to be alone. I was in an unfamiliar place and at a pivotal point in my life. It was pivotal because in four years I desperately needed to have acquired my degree. No, my family did not place any pressure on me, it was all pressure that I placed on myself. Not graduating in exactly four years was not an option! I wanted to make my dad and siblings proud. Most importantly, I wanted to have a "perfect" life. If I accomplished this phase of my education then I would be well on my way. However, life teaches you that there is no such thing as perfection. Boy, did I learn that the hard way.

As I stated earlier, my major was pre-med. I have always been fascinated with science and most importantly the human body. Knowledge of those things just came naturally to me. Or so I thought. Well, there was one class that literally knocked me off of my feet in a negative way. That class was Organic Chemistry. For the first time, I found myself struggling with school and spending a lot of time studying. Talk about feeling overwhelmed! I became so frustrated that I changed my major. Looking back over this period of my life, things did not have to transpire in this manner. I am sure that if I would have spoken to someone about my feelings, I would have continued to pursue pre-med. Most importantly, if my mom was still alive, I am almost certain that I would not have changed my major.

Struggling with that class caused me to subtly entertain the thought of not graduating from college. That thought caused me to make a very rash and nonsensical decision. In order for me to ensure that I successfully completed college, I changed my major to Psychology. My thought process was I could complete my coursework, graduate from college, and afterwards still attend medical school.

Psychology is the study of the mind and behavior. Instantly, I grew fond of my new major. It was like a breath of fresh air. I began to learn about all aspects of the human experience from child development to aging. The study of Psychology was what I needed to help me understand myself and others. It was also what I needed to begin the healing process from my mother's death. It wasn't until I began to study Psychology that I began to see the magnitude of the trauma that I had experienced and how that trauma shaped me into the person that I had become.

I was a broken individual. That brokenness affected my self-esteem. In 2 Timothy 1:7 it states, "For God hath not given us the spirit of fear; but of power, love, and of a sound mind." My brokenness caused me to fear getting close to people. I thought they would be taken away from me like my mom. On the other hand, the trauma that accompanied my mother's death gave me a strong will that helped me to never give up in the midst of adversity. In spite of all of the adversity that I experienced, I still had an inner drive and desire to become someone great that could reach back and help others.

I graduated from college with a BS in Psychology. My experiences during that time helped me learn that if I wanted to achieve something I had to work for it and that it is okay if it does not

THROUGH THE STORM

come easily. I thank God for these growing pains because they helped shape me into a God-fearing woman that acknowledges her shortcomings and setups for greatness.

Abortion

2002

Chapter 3

Life After College

In 2000, my dream of getting my degree came true. I wanted to celebrate my accomplishment, so I decided to go out with a friend and my baby sister the day before graduation. I attended an NFL fundraising party to celebrate. I was at the end of a long relationship and was ready to embrace my new beginning. I had not been out in a while with my girls, so I was super excited.

The party was crowded and filled with a lot of people having a good time. In spite of my mild-mannered personality, I've always enjoyed a great party with great music and great friends. Shortly after entering the party, a young man approached me and asked if I would like to dance. He was tall and very well dressed. I said sure. Well, we danced and talked pretty much the entire night. Prior to me leaving, we exchanged numbers.

After that night, James and I would talk on the phone daily for hours. We would talk about everything. He was a great conversationalist, which helped me out a lot. I began to enjoy his companionship. He was a big talker, but most importantly, a great listener. Ultimately we became great friends.

THROUGH THE STORM

As our friendship grew, we did so much together. He was a perfect gentleman and quite the romantic. He never pressured me about anything and was very generous with me. One thing that I really loved about him was that he adored me for me. I was excited and nervous about our relationship, but we took our time to get to know each other and did not rush into anything.

After a year of dating, we decided that we were officially a couple. During this time, I was trying to figure out the next phase in my life. I worked at Job Corps as a counselor while contemplating my next educational move. I confided in James about my aspirations. With his help, I eventually enrolled in graduate school to pursue my Masters in Education. Totally different path for me, but I was willing to try it.

Our relationship grew because I enjoyed our friendship. We could talk about anything and we enjoyed each other's company. Shortly after the official relationship began, the relations also began. All throughout college I was cautious and careful to protect myself in efforts to keep from getting pregnant. Once I started dating James, that caution went out of the window. As I stated, during this time, I was working and enrolled in graduate school. I finally felt like my life was flowing in a positive direction. However, I reached a bump in the road. In 2002, after a year of officially dating, I found out that I was pregnant.

I was so disappointed in myself. I was the first one in my immediate family to graduate from college and now I was the first one to enroll into graduate school. As I stated previously, I have always envisioned having a perfect life. I desired to get married and established before I got pregnant. I just did not understand how I could've been so careless at this point in my life. Everybody that knew me knew that I absolutely loved children, but I just felt like having a child at this time in my life was not what I needed.

A few weeks after finding out that I was pregnant, I started having morning sickness. It was something that I had never felt or experienced before and I hated it. I was so distracted by what I considered a fault that I could not see that the baby growing inside of me was a blessing from God. I was so busy focusing on myself that I could not see the positive at all in this situation. So many feelings overwhelmed me such as guilt, anger, frustration, confusion, and sadness.

"How could you be so careless?" I kept asking myself. The only way that I felt that I could deal with this issue was to terminate the pregnancy. Before making such a drastic decision, I did take the time to talk about my thoughts and feelings. On many instances, James and my family stated that I should not terminate the pregnancy and that they would assist me in taking care of my child. James was so excited about the pregnancy, but I just could not come to grips with it. I just felt so

horrible, not realizing that the situation would pass and that greatness would come out of this pregnancy. I was in a predicament that was caused by my impetuous behavior and I just did not know what to do.

As I stated, James was so excited about me being pregnant as well as his family. This would have been his parents' first grandchild. I now know that they would have been great grandparents, but I was just not ready for that huge responsibility.

Growing up without my mom placed such a huge damper in my life. I felt that if I could not give my all, then I did not want to give anything. I had so many negative thoughts flowing through my mind. The one thought that resonated the most with me was that it was not the right time. I felt James and I both were not emotionally or mentally ready to take care of a child. I was wrong for projecting my issues onto him. I never really took his feelings into consideration. It was just all about what I wanted or felt was necessary for me at the moment. James was disappointed in me and my decision. He heard what I said, but ultimately did not agree with it. James pleaded with me not to have an abortion, but I felt that it was not his decision to make because it was not his body; it was mine.

How can I be this person that appeared to be so well put together, yet in this dilemma? How had I made such a huge mistake and been so irresponsible to not protect myself?

I talked to James and my family multiples times about my decision; they all tried to discourage me from following through, but my mind was made up. Now that I look back, I was afraid of accepting responsibility for my actions and ultimately knew that it was wrong to have an abortion. I knew deep down that I was not making the right decision; however, I was focused on myself, my goals, and how my life would appear. I just could not see that this baby was a gift God, but life has a way of showing you the things that you should treasure. Like older, seasoned individuals always say, just keep living.

In Psalm 127:3 it states, "Children are a gift from the Lord; they are a reward from him." This scripture did not become real in my life until later.

On the day of my abortion, I was vexed. I was annoyed, irritated, and unsettled. I prayed and asked God to forgive me for what I was about to do. Why didn't I change my mind after praying? Honestly, I just did not see a way out. I had never faced or made any decisions of this magnitude before. I just did not have the faith that I needed to believe that I would have been okay if I would have kept my child. I wanted to be all that I could to my child; I did not want my child to feel what I felt. That was a life growing inside of me that I was supposed to protect. Instead, I made the decision to end that life due to my irresponsibility.

THROUGH THE STORM

I went to Planned Parenthood to have my abortion. I can say that I learned early on how to detach my feelings to keep from hurting. I developed that after my mom died. So, I laid on the table and asked God again to forgive me as that child's life was literally pulled out of me.

That abortion was the biggest mistake and regret of my life. I toiled and toiled with my decision, but I just did not see how I was going to make it through that situation. I just kept thinking about the fact that I did not want to struggle raising a child. It wasn't a financial issue, but I knew that I did not want to struggle mentally.

Now I know that was just a trick of the enemy. I should have just accepted my responsibility and continued with my pregnancy. The abortion was an easy fix, but the beginning of future obstacles and bumps in the road ahead.

Chapter 4

Life After My Biggest Regret

I learned early on how to let things go and detach myself from those things that hurt. I grieved for a little while and went on with my life. As I look back over my life, I now know that I never really grieved. I just suppressed my emotions and feelings which is a very unhealthy coping mechanism. It is unhealthy because the issue is never addressed and never truly goes away. I equated dealing with my issues on my own as being a strong person. I now know that I was really a weak person that added on layers and layers of hurt. Those layers of hurt ultimately caused me to lose myself.

Honestly, after having the abortion, I felt as if another void was created in my life. This void caused me to suffer a physical and mental pain that I did not and could not deal with. So instead of dealing with it, I said to myself, "Life goes on."

"It is over with" was the motto that I decided on. I was finished, in my mind, with the remnants of my abortion. So, two days after the abortion I was walking around as if things were back to normal. My oldest sister asked me if I was okay and I told her yes, but deep down inside I wasn't.

THROUGH THE STORM

I know that she knew that. She even questioned where I stood in my relationship with James. I did not respond. I can say that I was unsure about it and now admit that what I was going through was very hard to process, which is why I chose not to deal with it.

Although the abortion caused me to question a lot of things, James and I continued our relationship. There were a lot of issues that were unresolved because I just did not have the strength or energy to deal with them. James began to question my commitment to him and even wondered if infidelity was the reason why I chose to have the abortion. That was not the case at all and I expressed that to him. Early on in our relationship, I made the decision to always maintain a high level of openness and honesty. I never wanted him to have to guess how or what I was feeling, but during this evolving point in my life, I just couldn't. Uncertainty about the direction of our relationship was definitely something that I pondered.

One issue with our relationship, in particular, was trust. He did not understand why, all of the sudden, I did not trust him and his ability to care for our child. My reasoning was that I was just too independent and that it was nothing that he had done. It was a defense mechanism that I used to help me cope with life. I have always been accustomed to dealing with issues on my own to the point that I had never given others an opportunity to help me with them. I did not have to be that way because I had a loving and supportive family. However, I felt that if I did not involve others in my affairs, the chances of my situations becoming more complicated diminished. In other words, I did not want to come to grips with the disappointment of others if things did not pan out the way that I thought they should. It was an excuse that allowed me to accept my limitations. At this point, life taught me that excuses have a way of alleviating incapacity.

2003

1st Ectopic Pregnancy

Chapter 5

The Beginning of my Storm

After a couple of years of dating, James and I decided that we wanted to get married. I didn't want to just continue dating. I didn't just want to be an arm piece. I wanted to be a wife. Despite my biggest regret, I have always had a conservative view of family. I believe in the institution of marriage and because of that, I had no doubt that I wanted to and would get married. I honestly felt that once I got married, it would help erase the guilt that I felt from having an abortion.

As I mentioned earlier in the book, James and I never dealt with the abortion nor did we address the issues surrounding it. We were just haphazardly dating and now planning a wedding. Our once great communication skills had taken a turn for the worse. That was terrible because communication is essential for a successful marriage. We talked, but when it came to serious issues, we would only scratch the surface or disregard them altogether.

Not addressing your issues only places a bandage on them. The wounds are still present. When in a relationship, you have to learn to talk about what you are going through and learn to deal with things. When you don't, that leads to chaos. In other words, James and I were about to become entangled with dysfunction.

Also, I began to entertain the thought of having a child. I anticipated that the next time I became pregnant I would be married as well as mentally ready.

While planning for our wedding, I noticed something. It was around December 2003 and my menstrual cycle was late. Eager to see why, I decided to purchase a pregnancy test. I went home and tested myself. It was positive!

I told James that I was pregnant. We were both nervous and slightly excited about it, I guess. My wedding was 3 months away. I decided to keep the news just between us.

It was close to the Christmas holidays. I was working my full-time job and a part-time job at Macy's. Everybody who knew me knew that I loved to shop. I chose to work at Macy's during the holidays so that I could take advantage of the discount. One night while at work, I noticed that I had a slight pain in my pelvic area so I decided to take a break. I really did not think too much about it and did not know that this was a sign of an abnormal pregnancy.

After that happened I decided to inform one of my older sisters about my pregnancy. A few days afterward, that same sister told me about a dream that she had regarding this pregnancy. In the dream it appeared as if the baby was stuck in a tunnel and could not get out. Coincidentally, I had a similar dream. I found it rather strange, but I still did not think anything about it.

I scheduled an appointment and it was confirmed that I was pregnant. However, my doctor also informed me that the baby was not in my uterus, but was developing inside of my right fallopian tube. Not understanding anything about pregnancy, I naively thought the baby could be removed and placed into my uterus. The pregnancy would have to be terminated.

I did not pry or inquire about why the pregnancy transpired in that manner. I cooperated with my doctor and the pregnancy was terminated.

After that procedure, James and I did not talk about it. This was another event that created a void in my life. The trauma that I was experiencing caused me to become subtly numb. Little did I know, it was also affecting my future husband in the same way.

Another wound and emotionally taxing experience had taken place in our lives that was never dealt with. I dealt with it the same way that I dealt with my abortion; I was oblivious to it. Again, I stated to myself, "Life goes on." I just put on my mask and went on with life.

Yes, James and I were just going on with life. We never grieved the loss of these children. How crazy is that? You should always assess your circumstances and deal with your issues, otherwise you are a walking time bomb that is ready to explode.

The next few months, I focused on planning my wedding. The wedding took my mind off what I had experienced and gave me something positive to look forward to. I could finally have my wedding and begin having my children. Little did I know, my storm of infertility had just begun.

2nd Ectopic Pregnancy
(Removal of left fallopian tube)

2004

Chapter 6

What is Going On?

Months passed by and now it was March 2004; about two weeks before my wedding. I was really excited about it. Finally, I was getting ready to become a married woman. Most women dream about one day walking down the aisle and that dream was about to come true for me. My wedding was thoroughly planned and coordinated just like I wanted it. I finally felt like I was in a good space.

My body operated like clockwork. If anything seemed out of order, I immediately noticed. However, when I realized my cycle was late, I figured that maybe my body was just stressed. Just to be on the safe side, I purchased a pregnancy test.

I went to the doctor and it was confirmed that I was pregnant. Thoughts began to flow through my mind. I also noticed that I started to experience tension and anxiety after finding out the news. I did not want to experience another pregnancy loss. I had a regular visit which consisted of having blood drawn to check my hormone levels. My doctor told me to not think about my last pregnancy and tried to reassure me that this could turn out as a successful pregnancy. She did make the disclaimer that she could not make any promises. She also stated that she could not confirm its viability in this instance until she rechecked my levels. *Viability* and *hormone levels* were phrases that were beginning to stand out to me. Fear began to well up inside of me. James shared the same emotions, including nervousness and anxiety. We were told to come back in to the doctor's office in a couple of days to have my blood levels rechecked. I was further informed that if my blood levels remained low, that was indicative of a possible pregnancy issue.

After our doctor's visit, James and I agreed that we were going to refocus on our wedding. I did however, go back to the doctor the day before our wedding to have lab work done. After that, I tried not to think about the pregnancy.

Later that night, I had a bachelorette party. My sister and friends really laid it out for me. This was my last day as a single woman and I was supposed to have the time of my life. I tried, but couldn't. As we were riding downtown, I began to experience pelvic pain. I told one of my friends about it and she stated that was normal during pregnancy. I considered that, but then I had a flashback of my last pregnancy where I experienced similar pelvic pain. I blotted out the thought and tried to enjoy myself, but I honestly couldn't, so we ended the night early. My excuse was that I needed to get some rest before my big day.

I woke up early the next day, nervous as ever. I knew that this was going to be the day that my life changed forever. My wedding was absolutely beautiful. I was glad to share it with my friends and family. It was all that I imagined. Although I was excited about our wedding, I was extremely nervous and uncertain about my lab results.

After my wedding, I was exhausted. James and I did not get much rest because a few hours after getting home and settled, we were headed for our honeymoon.

We went on a seven-day cruise. The entire time I felt horrible. I felt like the bottom of my stomach was going to fall apart. The entire time I experienced severe bleeding, nausea, and pelvic pain. What was supposed to be the most exciting time of my life was the exact opposite.

Upon returning from our honeymoon, I noticed that someone had left me a voicemail. It was my ob-gyn. She left a message on the Monday after my wedding. She stated that I was not to go on my honeymoon and to report to her office ASAP. After hearing the message, I called the office and was told to report to the hospital immediately! I'll say that again; not her office, but the hospital.

My anxiety went into overload. I did not understand the sense of urgency. I was shocked, hurt, afraid, and confused. James was also confused but he was right there with me. I called my dad, siblings, and a close friend and informed them of the news. They told me that they were on their way. I told them to pray for me because I was really unsure about what was happening.

THROUGH THE STORM

One thing that I can say for sure is that I have a praying family and prayer is what sustained me through all of this. They were and are always there during trying times such as this.

After entering the hospital, I was told that I had to have an emergency surgery. It was as if I walked through the hospital door, was given the news, and then blanked out. When I awoke, I was told that my left fallopian tube was removed. My doctor stated that the baby had grown in my fallopian tube and the tube ruptured. This is called an ectopic pregnancy. I was shown pictures that were quite disturbing to me, but I still did not understand the specifics surrounding ectopic pregnancies. My doctor further informed me that the baby had grown to the size of a plum. I can visualize the pictures now. I felt so overwhelmed, numb, and confused.

Lastly, my doctor told me that if I would have waited any longer my fallopian tube would have ruptured and I would have possibly bled to death. My eyes got so big that I know they looked as if they were going to pop out.

Questions began to overwhelm my mind. What was going on with my body? Why was this happening? What was causing this? Will this happen again?

The first faces that I saw after the surgery were James, my step-mom, and my wedding coordinator. Boy, was I glad to see them. They prayed for me and gave me some encouraging words. After that I felt a sense of gratitude. I was thankful that God spared my life. Although I was thankful, I felt quite perplexed. My reality was becoming present. In the past I overlooked my issues, now I was beginning to see them at face value. I almost felt as if I was reliving the hurt of my abortion. However, this hurt was different. Now that I was married and ready to have a child, I was experiencing pregnancy issues. What was going on?

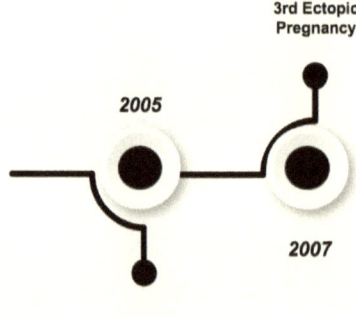

Chapter 7

Longing for What I Couldn't Have

In 2005, I had been married roughly about a year and a half. Although James and I dated for 4 years, you can say that we were getting to know each other as a married couple. I tell people that are not married, jokingly, that you don't really get to know a person until you live with them. That is a true statement! Marriage is truly for mature people and age is not the determining factor.

I was in the newlywed phase of my marriage. According to society, "First comes love, then comes marriage, and then comes the lady with the baby carriage." When things don't happen how society says it should, it is deemed or looked upon as being fragmented. Living up to society's expectations can make a person feel out of joint. In other words, you are made to feel like something is wrong with you.

At this moment in time, I can say that I was longing for a child. Several of my close friends had a child or were expecting. I can honestly say that a small root of jealousy began to grow inside of me because of my infertility. I was not jealous of them personally because I loved my friends. However, I was jealous because of what their body was capable of doing that mine seemingly couldn't. I wanted to experience being pregnant. I wanted to have children so that our children could grow up together. Ultimately, I wanted to be able to have a child with my husband.

During this time, my husband and I purchased our first home. It was beautiful. We were accomplishing pretty much everything that we thought we were supposed to accomplish at this time. So, now that we had our house, we felt that it was time to have our children.

James and I joined a new church. It was our saving grace. Our pastor was a great teacher. He taught about biblical truths that were practical, necessary, and most importantly, life-changing. Although we were attending this Bible-based church, we were still experiencing some issues. I notice the changes subtly. James was becoming slightly irritable and withdrawn. We began to argue about minor concerns.

Sincerely, I wanted to become the best wife that I could be. I wanted a great marriage and never wanted divorce to be an option. There were many things that I wanted to attain in life and I was trying to make those things happen in my own strength. In my own strength, huh? Totally impossible.

On top of that, we still had the issue of infertility floating in the background. James started to press the matter surrounding us having children, so we decided that we would try. It had been over a year since my last pregnancy, so why not? In addition to us trying, we should have taken the time to address our past by going through some form of counseling, but we didn't.

I began to pray for our marriage. My husband and I were still experiencing communication issues and now the current fertility issues. We were stressed to say the least. I began to study the word of God because I knew that my life was a mess. I was hurting and just plain frustrated.

This was my second year teaching school. I enjoyed teaching, but I will say that I was not the most pleasant nor nurturing. I just did not have that gift in me, so most of the time I was not empathetic towards my students and their needs. I was a great disciplinarian and could really make learning interesting, but if they had a problem, they just had to find a way to deal with it. Sounds familiar? I was expecting them to deal with their issues the same way that I had dealt with mine.

Due to my current circumstances, hurt and bitterness began to take root in my heart. In order to deal with my negative emotions, I would just wear a mask. I began really studying the word of God. I realized that I needed some help with processing my life. Instead of focusing on inner healing, I just continued to focus on prayers for my marriage, mainly because I attributed my hurt to my marriage. I desired to be a good wife, eventually a good parent, and ultimately a good person. I was smiling on the outside, yet unhappy on the inside.

THROUGH THE STORM

In the meantime, I got pregnant again. As it has been made known, I desperately longed for a child, but the lack of being able to have a successful pregnancy caused me to experience great inner turmoil. I immediately got into routine: Positive pregnancy test at home, next make an ob-gyn appointment.

I made an appointment for the next day. Lab work was done to check my blood levels. I also had an ultrasound. I found that it was odd that I had to have one, but this time I was further along than the past two pregnancies. When the ultrasound was done, guess what? We saw a sac in the uterus. My doctor told me to come back in a week to have my blood levels rechecked. The news seemed promising, but my gut felt something different. This time I waited to tell James that I was pregnant because I hoped that this third time things would work out. God knows that I hoped that things would turn out well! Since I had been through a couple of failed pregnancies, my faith at this point and time was very limited.

Well, the embryo made it to my uterus. When I returned home from my appointment, I decided to share the news with James. I shared it because I hoped that this time we would have a positive outcome. He did not say much, but I know that he hoped for the same. I went back to the doctor a week later to have my blood levels rechecked.

My ob-gyn was optimistic.

"Third times a charm," she said.

TERRINY LLOYD

I was told to come back in a week to check for a fetal heartbeat. All the constant returning to the doctor's office was becoming agitating and dreadful. I dreaded it because I was afraid of how things would turn out. So, in a week's time, I returned and had another ultrasound. We did not see or hear a fetal heartbeat. The nurse took me back to the room and said that my doctor would be with me shortly. My heart dropped. I knew what that meant all too well. Once again, I was receiving bad news.

My doctor came in and told me that the pregnancy would have to be terminated. She stated that I had what was called a blighted ovum. In other words, a sac developed but a baby didn't. At this point, I was beyond frustrated and confused. Why was this happening to me?

Infertility not only took a toll on me, but it also took a toll on my marriage. My husband began to express his hurt about our infertility. Not only was I hurt because of what I was going through, I was also hurt because I did not have an understanding husband. He could not understand why we were not able to have children.

"If you would not have had an abortion, we would have children now," he said.

Wow, that was a low blow. I always felt that no matter what you face in a marriage, a husband and wife should be understanding towards each other. However, that was not the case. We would argue all the time about this. It occurred so much that it really began to put a strain on our marriage that should have ended up in either separation or divorce.

Why was I experiencing failure at the point of a breakthrough? Was I being punished for the abortion that I had?

If I want something, I go hard to try to attain it. That is how I ended up dealing with my onset infertility. I became infatuated with becoming pregnant and having a child. It began to consume my thoughts and my life.

All my life I longed to become a mother. These unfortunate experiences damaged my emotions and my confidence as a woman. I felt ashamed and embarrassed.

Despite my brokenness, that shame was what I used to persevere through my circumstances. It was like I would hurt for the moment and then I would let it go.

As I began to study the word, I learned that it was God's will for us to be fruitful and to multiply. After learning that, I refused to let that promise go, even though it was evident that my husband did not believe it. I came in agreement with that word. I would say to myself that it was God's will for me to have children.

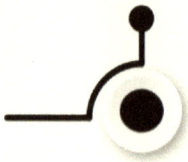

4th Ectopic Pregnancy

2011

Chapter 8

The Storm of My Life

We dealt with fertility issues and now marital issues. The storms of my life were definitely raging. My storm was filled with indifference and conflicts. It produced heavy clouds of burden that followed me for a large portion of my life. Although my life was not always gloomy, those storm clouds helped me begin to see what I was made of. I was very fragile and vulnerable. Through that vulnerability, I learned who I was. I was desperately broken, almost to the point of no return. The warmth and coldness of my life caused heavy precipitation of trials, which sometimes made me question if God was with me. As I weathered my storms, I realized that He was with me because I did not lose it.

I spoke the word of God over my life and marriage. The word of God was powerful and imminent in my life. It opened my eyes and allowed to me to grow in more areas than one. Although at times, I was unable to see or figure out which direction I needed to take in life, I would always remember that storms do not last always and that God had me. He was the captain of my life.

My life was a storm filled with thunder, lightening, and heavy winds. My abortion, miscarriages, and ectopic pregnancies were all forms of thunder. Those events were fearful, but afterwards they would cause me to sit still and reflect. The lightening represented the conflicts that I experienced within myself and with my husband. Those conflicts would shed a light on my darkest moments and enabled me to see that all things eventually come to the light.

I realized that I had to deal with my internal and external conflicts because they were not going away. Lastly, I experienced heavy winds. Those were life situations, things, and people that gave me the strength that I needed to endure. God, my family, friends, and successes in life were my wind. These were my anchors that held me down and kept me balanced.

Storms are hard to endure especially when it seems that they are causing a plethora of destruction in your life. However, my storms allowed me to see my strengths and weaknesses. My storm was my saving grace.

Chapter 9

Growing Pains

In life, most people do not like to share their hurt with others, but I had to. For years, I kept so many of the intricate details of my life bottled up inside that I had to let them out. I could no longer hide under a mask nor mask my emotions. I wanted to be free. Free to live, free to grow, and free to let go!

In life, you go through different phases; some good, some bad. Those phases are your life cycles that ultimately lead to growth. I began to see growth in many areas. For example, I began to acknowledge my faults within myself. The first path to healing is definitely when you can acknowledge your faults. Not only did I acknowledge them, but I addressed them.

I had to learn to become comfortable in my own skin. If I didn't love me, then who else would? My happiness was my priority. I was not responsible for other people's happiness. I got to a place where I no longer valued how others felt about me more than how I valued myself. The less I worried about being accepted by others, the less pressure I experienced.

Most importantly, as I matured I began to see and understand that God had a plan for me. I just had to trust the process. Although it may have appeared to others that my destiny was to remain infertile, I knew that God have a plan for my pain. Those painful experiences helped to birth my destiny. In Jeremiah 29:11, it states, "For I know the plans that I have for you. Plans to prosper you and bring you to an expected end." I did not know how God was going to work out my life, but I knew that He had a plan and that I would come out on top in the end.

Chapter 10

Counseling, Are You Serious?

One of my prayers was that God would heal my marriage. Due to our seemingly irreconcilable differences, James and I decided to go to counseling. We knew that we needed to get a handle on our marriage, so we decided that counseling would be good for the both of us. Deep down I knew that he wanted our marriage to work just as much as I did.

Both of us were really close to our families. He was especially close to his dad; they were best friends. James would talk to him daily about everything, even our marriage. He informed his dad that we were thinking about going to counseling.

"Don't go in there telling those people all of your business," his dad said.

We attended our first session on a Saturday morning. I can remember it like it was yesterday. The counselor started asking us questions. When I would speak, she would nod or make a statement as if she was in agreement with everything that I said. On the other hand, when James would speak, she would ask questions. Basically, she made him feel like what he said and did was wrong. So, after about the third or fourth question, James began to give the counselor the side-eye.

Finally, James asked the counselor if could he ask her a question, she replied yes.

"Have you ever been married?"

"No."

He then stated that the session was over and walked out. That was the first and last time that we attended. I can laugh about this now, but at the time it wasn't funny.

I asked God what to do next. I began to purchase books about marriage. I had to find a way to fill those voids that had developed in my life. It appeared that I was trying to use my husband, my career, and even having a child to make me feel complete. So, I began to work on me. Sometimes in life we try to use people and/or things to complete us. I learned the hard way that being whole has nothing to do with others, but everything to do with me.

I got involved in my church and connected with some strong women that would pray for me and stand in the gap for me. I shared my experiences with many people. Just when I would get ready to lose hope, God would send people across my path that would encourage me to not give up. I can remember my best friend telling me that she had dreams of me with children. Another friend would call me every time that I got pregnant. I had a couple of individuals prophesy that I would have children or speak encouraging words over my life.

I had countless people who prayed for me. God would always send a sign to reassure me that He did not and would not forget about me.

My pastor really had a passion to help married couples. Boy, that was exactly what we needed at this point in our life. This church and its teachings helped my marriage. He and his wife would talk about marriage and we both felt that they were speaking directly to us.

Although I was praying for my marriage, the healing of my marriage was not instant. We still argued, we were still distant and had communication issues, and we still did not have any children! In spite of what we were going through, I had to remember that God had a plan.

My storms were maturing me and I did not even realize it. They were used to nourish my soul because I needed to grow up spiritually and mentally. They also helped me cleanse the air by allowing me to see that I had to let go of my negative mindset to develop a new perspective of life in a Godly way so that I could finally breathe.

Chapter 11

A Blessing in the Midst of Disappointment

Before God blesses you, He oftentimes must heal you. He has to heal you from your past before He births in you something new. A new beginning was something that I needed at this point in my life.

I began to ask God for healing; spiritually, mentally, and emotionally. I would pray healing scriptures over my body daily. I also began to ask God to deliver me from toxic emotions that I had towards myself and others. Lastly, I prayed that God would remove all spiritual, physical, and emotional blockages in my life.

In the midst of what I call my spiritual cleansing, I got pregnant. I was excited after I saw the positive pregnancy test. However, the excitement was short lived. Why? Because I began to experience some of the same symptoms that I experienced in past pregnancics. Unlike in the past, I began to pray over my body and ask that God's will be done.

I went to the doctor and had the regular formalities done: ultrasound, blood work, etc. Each time I would anticipate seeing something in my uterus. When the ultrasound was done, again, nothing was visible. As time passed, I got the news that I had another ectopic pregnancy.

Was I disappointed? Absolutely, but I just knew and believed that God had a plan. My faith had definitely increased as well as my expectation in what He could do in my life. I was blessed in the midst of my disappointment. In Philippians 4:6-7 it states, *"Don't worry about anything; instead, pray about everything. Tell God what you need, and thank him for all he has done. Then you will experience God's peace, which exceeds anything we can understand. His peace will guard your hearts and minds as you live in Christ Jesus" (NLT).*

Chapter 12

A Change has Come

This time in my life brought a lot of questions and reflection. I began to do a lot of soul searching. Was I being punished for something that I had done? Why didn't my body behave the way that it was supposed to when I became pregnant? I longed for days to be called Mother or Mommy.

I began to research abortions and the harmful effects that they could have on your body. I learned that abortions could cause sterility or scarring of your fallopian tubes. My fallopian tubes were scarred and had to heal.

I began to ask God to forgive me of past and present sins as I continued to work on me. I was accepted into a leadership program that I had previously tried to get into multiples times. I was really excited about the change in direction that my life was going in. At this point, my marriage was getting better. We were moving forward, yet there were some things that we were still working through.

My life was seemingly lining up. I was in a good place, for real this time. One day as I was driving down the street, the Lord dropped the name of this book in my spirit. At first, I wondered how I was going to write this book and I didn't have any children. I called my sister, Janice, who is an evangelist and shared the news with her. She was overjoyed.

"God is just giving you another one of His many signs that He is going to answer your prayers," she said. Janice ended the call by saying, "Get excited and rejoice!"

I was happy because it gave me hope. It helped reignite that mustard seed of faith that I needed to continue to believe that God was going to restore me, like He had done many times during my storm. Whenever I felt like giving up on having children, He would always send someone or something my way to encourage me.

During this time, I visited a fertility specialist that I had gone to before. In the previous visit, I did not receive any concrete reasoning to explain my infertility. I wanted to visit one again just to see if I could get some help or an explanation as to why I was experiencing infertility. After my visit, the specialist told me that he still saw some scar tissue on my fallopian tube and if I tried to conceive again it was possible that I could have another ectopic pregnancy. However, he also stated that he wanted to help. He wanted to place my name on a list to see if I would qualify for in-vitro fertilization. James and I had talked about it but were worried about the cost and the actual chances of it working. My specialist further stated that I would probably qualify for a program for women who had suffered multiple miscarriages. If

I was approved for the study, I would only have to pay 20 percent of the cost. I thought that the Lord had finally smiled on me and answered my prayers. Maybe now I will finally have children.

    My girlfriends and I decided to take a cruise which was much needed for me. I needed some time away from everything. I needed time away from my husband, time away from dealing with my infertility, and time away from the stresses of life. The cruise took place during hurricane season, so the water was rocky. Many people got sick from the cruise, but I didn't. I just adapted to my situation. It was almost like the hurricane represented my life and God was telling me that I needed to have peace during the storm. Even in the midst of the storm, I learned to find a way to remain calm. Having some time to myself helped me and my marriage. I was able to pull away from my stressors and remove more toxicity out of my life.

    Time passed and I had not heard from the fertility specialist, so I decided to give him a call. I really anticipated some great news. After speaking to the nurse, my heart dropped. She told me that I did not qualify for the program because I had too many miscarriages! Really? I thought that was what the program was set up for. I reminded myself that God had a plan. I needed strength after that call and God gave it to me.

    "I will be a mother one day," I told myself.

THROUGH THE STORM

In Philippians 4:13 it states, "I can do all things through Christ that strengthens me."

**Positive
Pregnancy**

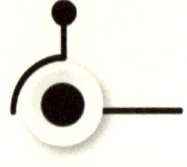

2012

Chapter 13

Facing Reality

Although I had faith, I began to accept the fact that maybe I was not going to have children. I decided to explore options including adoption, but in my heart I did not want to do that. I wanted to birth my own children and I still had that mustard seed of faith that I would. I just had to face my reality.

I spoke with my ob-gyn regarding what my fertility specialist told me.

"Well, we're just going to keep trying," he said. I looked surprised and could not believe that he said that. God used my doctor to encourage me to keep trying because He knew the plan that He had for me.

A couple of months passed, and my cycle was late.

"Oh, Lord," I said to myself. *"Here we go again."*

I immediately went to the store to purchase a pregnancy test. I did not wait to take it at home, I took it at the store. This time my results looked different. I had a feeling that things were going to be different. I did not tell my husband because of everything that we had gone through in the past. I did not need to deal with any negativity or doubt.

Later that day, my husband had to speak at my brother-in law's church. I noticed when I was sitting in the audience he kept staring at me. After service, I asked him why.

"I think you are pregnant," he said. I kept the fact that he was right to myself. "I think you need to go and get a pregnancy test to see if you are." I finally told him about the test I had already taken. "I knew it!" he said. "You need to make an appointment." The next day, I did.

When I arrived at my appointment, I just had a feeling that things were going to go right this time. I was going to have this baby! The formalities were done; BP check, urine and blood sample, and lastly an ultrasound. Anxiety began to creep in, but I took a deep breath and calmed down.

The room was cold and dark. The nurse came and began the scans, typing information as she took photos. This was totally different from other ultrasounds that I had done. We asked if could she see anything. She said there was a sac. This was good news because with my last pregnancies we could not see anything.

Our next hurdle was to see if we would hear a heartbeat. We were told to come back in two weeks to see if a heartbeat could be detected. That was the longest wait ever. Guess what? When we returned, we heard a heartbeat. It was beating 160 bpm. My husband and I were so excited! The very thing that we waited for finally happened. James was so excited that he stated that this news was the best Christmas gift that he had in such a long time. This was truly a miracle, my miracle!

It took several years for me to have a viable pregnancy, but it happened. I learned that everything happens in God's timing.

My pregnancy progressed fine, until one day as I was attending a prenatal visit, my doctor asked me if I was feeling okay. He said that my blood pressure was really high and wondered if he needed to send me to the hospital. I told him no, my blood pressure would go down on its own. I had another prenatal visit a few weeks later and my blood pressure was up again. This time I was referred to a high-risk specialist. With this doctor, I would have to go for bi-monthly visits to make sure that my pregnancy was progressing normally with my pre-eclampsia.

My pregnancy was monitored by my ob-gyn and the high-risk doctor. At my last prenatal visit, my blood pressure was 160/120. My doctor asked me to sit for an hour so that he could monitor it. Well, it never went down. I was admitted into the hospital and had my baby the next day. My baby was born 1 pound and 7 ounces. The scariest time of my life.

I named her Haley Grace. I chose the name Haley because it meant hero. I chose the middle name Grace because I felt that God granted us the grace to have her. His grace would continuously be upon me and my child's life. God supernaturally blessed me to become a mother.

2013

Birth of First Child

Chapter 14

Sufficient Grace

My daughter was a micro preemie. Since I had never experienced going through anything like this, I did not know the challenges that I was about to face. My baby's lungs were not fully developed so she had to be placed on a breathing machine to assist her with breathing. This condition is called bronchopulmonary dysplasia. This condition can cause the child's lungs to grow abnormally or become inflamed. My baby's lungs were inflamed. I would watch her breathe and sometimes forget to breathe, because I would get so nervous when watching her. I oftentimes felt helpless, but I knew I had to be strong for my child.

I would pump breast milk to take to the hospital. Her body needed pure nourishment and I felt like that was something I could give to help her fragile body grow. Well, one night I received a frightening call. I was told that my child had blood in her stool and they were running tests to determine the cause. The test results stated that my daughter developed necrotizing enterocolitis. This condition is scarring of the intestines. Her feedings had to be stopped and she was placed on hospital nutrients.

My daughter dealt with jaundice and other issues. Another serious issue that she experienced was her heart did not develop fully. My baby had two holes in her heart. She was given medicine to close them, but the medicine did not work. After a month in a half after Haley's birth, she had to have surgery. I was devastated! Why did my baby have to go through so much? I loved the hospital that she was at, but she had to be transferred to the local children's hospital. I cried and cried but was given great advice from the nurses. They told me to always document what was going on with my baby and make sure that I was my baby's advocate. If I did not speak up for my baby, then who would?

Haley's surgery was successful. God's grace was upon my child. My baby spent 3 long months is the hospital, but she is now healthy and whole.

Birth of Second Child

2014

Chapter 15

Double for your Trouble

Despite all of the things that I went through with my first daughter, I knew that I wanted more than one child. I just had crazy faith like that. I did not plan on getting pregnant but if it happened I would be okay with it. A year and a half after my first child, I was pregnant again. I went to the doctor, they saw a sac. At the next appointment, they heard a heartbeat. The doctor was in awe due to only having one fallopian tube and all the miscarriages that I had.

"You must be living right because God has smiled on you and blessed you with another gift of life."

With everything that I went through with my first birth, I was monitored very closely. I was again referred to a high-risk specialist to monitor my blood pressure. Around my 6th month, I had an appointment and my blood pressure was very high. I was told to go the hospital where I remained for 8 weeks. I given so much medicine that I prayed it would not affect my baby.

While on bedrest, I dealt with multiple challenges including pre-eclampsia. Several times my blood pressure would be as high as 220/120. I did not understand what was going on with my body.

I rested a lot while in the hospital but that did not stop my condition. The doctors monitored me closely because having high blood pressure numbers like that could lead to a seizure or a stroke.

One day while getting an ultrasound, the high-risk doctor walked in and said my baby was not growing like she needed to be. They needed to deliver her. My second child was born at 30 weeks. She was 2 pounds.

Despite all the medicine that I was given, my baby did not have any issues. All she had to do was grow. She was not placed on any breathing machines, the only issue she experienced was jaundice. Glory to God! She was in the hospital for 6 weeks. I named her Adelynn Faith because I had to have faith to believe that I would have her and faith that she would be perfectly healthy. God answered my prayers.

Chapter 16

After the Storm

Infertility was a storm that I endured for many years. I went through years of despair, disappointment, confusion, and anger. I did not understand why I had to go through this storm, but when God dropped the name of this book in my spirit before I had kids, I knew that He was up to something.

In Genesis 30:1 it states, "And when Rachel saw that she bare Jacob no children, Rachel envied her sister; and said unto Jacob, Give me children, or else I die." In the beginning of my storm with infertility, I felt like Rachel. No, I am not saying that I was suicidal, but I felt that pain of desiring to have children with my husband and not being able to do so. The word states that the prayers of the righteous avail much. I prayed fervently to God and He healed all of my wounds.

God brought me through my storm, but I had to go through it for a while. My prayer was not answered instantaneously.

When we go through a storm, many times we ask, why me? We go through storms because there are some valuable lessons that we have to learn. Those lessons, or birthing pains, help shape us for our present and our future.

You must trust God despite how your situation looks. I learned that in life there are seasons, but the bad ones don't last always.

The trials taught me how to put my life into perspective. I learned to value the gift of life, because there were times that I could have lost mine. God taught me how to love myself because if I didn't learn that, how could I learn to love my children?

The joy that I developed permeates from a good place. The world did not give it and the world cannot take it away. I learned to have joy, even if my circumstances suggest otherwise.

I learned in all things, give thanks. I especially developed a heart of gratitude for the individuals that God allowed to be in my life such as my family, friends, coworkers, and even bosses. Without their support, I would have never made it through this journey.

Lastly, I learned that God is faithful and that He will give us the desires of our heart. Why? Because He loves us just that much. He extends His grace and mercy upon us and it is nothing that we have to do to get it. He is always with us as we weather our storms. In the end, the downpour of His rain helps us grow and birth something beautiful that can only come from Heaven above.

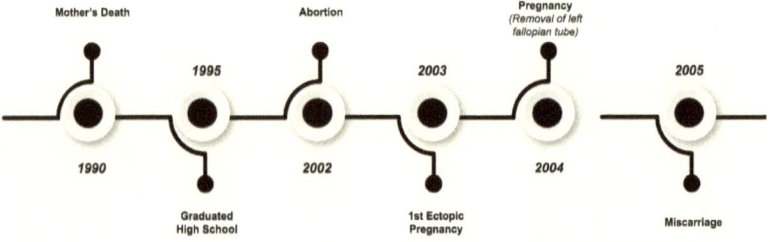

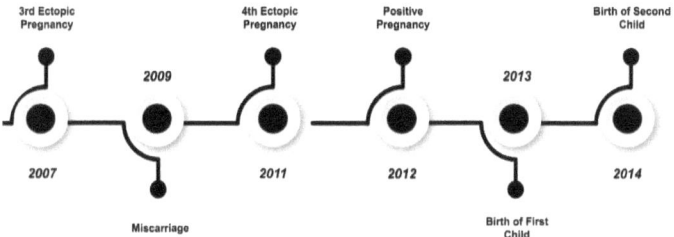

Terriny Lloyd is a devout Christian, wife, mother, and educator. She is loyal and has a heart for people that enables her to demonstrate a selfless love towards those that are hurting or in need. Her willingness to help others is motivated by her aspiration to see individuals grow into the person that God created them to be. Most importantly, she is an advocate for the underdog, because she knows that through proper nurturing and guidance, each individual can develop into a beautiful diamond that permeates beauty, resilience and love.

Contact Terriny at terrinyknox@yahoo.com.

www.ingramcontent.com/pod-product-compliance
Lightning Source LLC
Chambersburg PA
CBHW030457010526
44118CB00011B/973